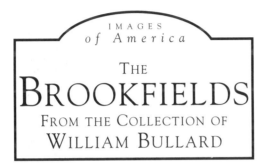

IMAGES
of America

THE
BROOKFIELDS
FROM THE COLLECTION OF
WILLIAM BULLARD

A Boston & Albany commuter train.

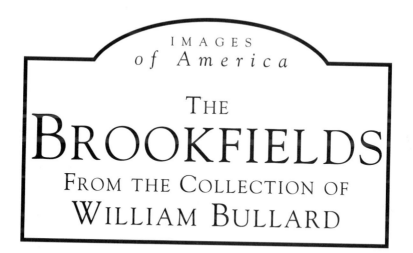

IMAGES
of America

THE
BROOKFIELDS
FROM THE COLLECTION OF
WILLIAM BULLARD

Dennis LeBeau

ARCADIA

First published 1996
Copyright © Dennis LeBeau, 1996

ISBN 0-7524-0294-3

Published by Arcadia Publishing,
an imprint of the Chalford Publishing Corporation
One Washington Center, Dover, New Hampshire 03820
Printed in Great Britain

Contents

To Paul and Thomas

Introduction

The known details of Bill Bullard's life are as spare and unblinking as his photographs. We know that William Stuart Bullard was born in Worcester, Massachusetts, in 1876, the eldest son of Ellen M. Barrett of Thomson (sic), Connecticut, and Charles E. Bullard of Worcester. We also know that he took his life in 1918 at the age of forty-one—this much is gleaned from his death certificate. "Cause of death," it reads without comment: "Suicide by hanging." "Test confirming diagnosis: view." "Place of death: North Brookfield, Massachusetts"—on the family farm where he was raised.

Not much is known about what motivated this driven itinerant photographer. One can imagine Bullard as a young man riding tirelessly across the New England countryside on his bicycle with a huge camera and cumbersome gear strapped to his back. Although the introduction of commercially available dry glass plates had simplified the process of taking pictures a great deal, itinerant photography remained an athletic undertaking in Bullard's time. Delicate strength and balance were required to pass over mostly dirt roads, and Bullard's baggy trousers and broad bicycle tires undoubtedly had the effect of molasses on a single-gear chain.

Despite this, Bullard was a prolific photographer, as his legacy of nearly five thousand glass negatives attests. He made his living from a small portrait studio at 5 Mayfield Street in Worcester, but his true passion lay in photographing New England towns and landscapes. He was particularly fascinated by the advance of technology; a large part of his collection is devoted to steam trains, factories, and shipyards. The overall range of the collection is extremely broad, however, evidencing Bullard's devotion to his art. In this compilation, his photographs document country life in the Brookfields at the turn of the century, preserving for posterity images of children and families, town halls, train stations, churches, factories, and schools. Almost every negative in the Bullard archive is a masterpiece of photographic composition; the photographer's pictures, in contrast to the convoluted course of his personal life, remain mirror smooth and crystalline clear.

The mystery of Bill Bullard's suicide in 1918 remains for the modern observer of his photographs to contemplate. The photographer's mother succumbed to cancer just two weeks before her son's hanging, and it seems likely that this event precipitated Bill's profound distress. Certainly other factors may have contributed to Bill's demise, however; concerning these, one may only speculate. Was his business failing, and had it become a struggle to make ends meet? Did his artistic vision, his fascination with a changing era, alienate him from his peers? Was he worn out from the sheer physical effort of creating so many painstaking images? In the absence of a personal diary, we have only the haunting faces and expressions of Bill and the Bullard family to ponder.

It was Charlie, the youngest Bullard boy, who had the foresight to save Bill's negatives from oblivion. He kept them safe for forty years, until photography enthusiast and local historian Frank Gaudette of East Brookfield purchased the collection in 1958. Frank passed the negatives and his love of photography on to his grandsons, Dennis and Robert LeBeau, and Dennis has maintained the archive in his own home.

A very small number of these images were made into postcards by Bullard; the overwhelming majority have never before been published.

One
East Brookfield

Our visit to East Brookfield starts appropriately at the depot. Designed by H.H. Richardson of Boston, this structure was erected by the Boston & Albany Railroad in 1894. It still serves as a railroad building.

Depot Square. In the center are Vizard's Drugstore and Opera House. The Keith Block, which serves today as East Brookfield's town hall, is on the right.

Depot Square. The dining room stood near the train station, next to the Keith Block.

Vizard's Drugstore and Opera House. The rear of the drugstore housed the Hotel Pilgrim.

Mechanic Street, looking west.

Pleasant Street. These three buildings serve today as the Meat and Spirit Shoppe, Brookfield Group Realty, and the Senior Center.

Pleasant Street, looking west. The photographer was standing on Mill Street.

One Cottage Street. The author of this volume currently resides here; it was also the home of Frank Gaudette.

The Lakeview House, on the site of the present-day Lashaway Inn, on Main Street.

The center of East Brookfield, from the corner of Cottage and Main Streets, looking west.

Main Street in the center of town, looking east. Fashionably dressed businessmen await the next trolley.

The Seminole. Once a boardinghouse, this building still stands atop the hill on Main Street. It is now an apartment complex.

Cottage Street in the winter, as seen from the Lakeview House.

Winter at Evergreen and Main Streets. This property was long known as the Wagner Farm. It was operated by Donald and Blanche Wagner and noted for its delicious strawberries and farm-fresh corn.

Varney's Garage on Main Street. It is now the site of Parson's Auto, where a Model T Ford can still be expertly serviced.

The home of Dr. William Hayward at Church and Main Streets. His choice of car? The Model T, of course. The family of Dr. and Mrs. Leonard Simonelli now live at this site. Church Street has been renamed Connie Mack Drive.

Saint John's Church. Formerly the District #8 schoolhouse, this building became East Brookfield's first Catholic place of worship. It was purchased from the town in 1891.

The East Brookfield Baptist Church on Main Street. Two young ladies pass along the road in front in their best Sunday dresses.

A view of the Baptist church. This was made into a popular postcard by William Bullard.

The Hotel Willena, at Main and South Streets.

Main Street, looking east, from the site of the present-day Ken's Citgo.

Main Street, looking east.

Main Street, again looking east. North Street is at the lower left; the house shown here stood on the site of Ken's Citgo.

A turn-of-the-century equivalent of the delivery truck. This horse and buggy carted groceries in East Brookfield.

A springtime view of Main Street, looking east.

Built to last. This sturdy brick home was built on West Main Street by B.W. Potter. It still stands today.

A home on North Street, now the residence of Reverend John Lindsay.

Lakeside recreation. Although the mechanics of boating have changed over the past century, summer fun at Lake Lashaway has not. Setting sail isn't always an easy task, as shown below.

A bird's eye view. The images on pp. 26–28 are panoramic views of East Brookfield, taken by Bill Bullard from Vizard's Hill on Howe Street. Hodgkins School is in the center of this photograph.

The center of town. Bridge Street is on the right; the Stevens Mill complex is in the foreground.

Four streets. Howe Street is in the foreground. Across the pond is Water Street, then Pleasant Street, and then Main Street.

Two views of Vizard's Opera House. This was the home of vaudeville entertainment in East Brookfield.

Fuel delivery. Wood and coal were delivered to East Brookfield homes by Alexander Coville. His wagon is shown here on the Fairbanks scale at the coal office in the freight yard.

Another load of wood ready to roll. The building in the background was the Boston & Albany Railroad engine house in East Brookfield.

Hauling cargo. Freight cars from North Brookfield are shown here being pushed to the main line. This photograph was taken from the North Brookfield branch-line bridge over the Five-Mile River.

A New England winter scene. Everyone pitches in to open the trolley line after a heavy snow.

Flag-Raising Day, April 28, 1917. The location is Mechanic Street, and the featured speaker was Lieutenant Governor Calvin Coolidge.

Dressed for the occasion. This is the interior of the East Brookfield Baptist Church, decorated for flag ceremonies.

A Podunk School entry in the Flag-Raising Day Parade. On the float, from left to right, are: Delbert Stone, Marion Menard, Lillian Menard, Millie Nichols, Anna Moynagh (standing), Louise Menard, Blanche Nichols, Donald Terry, Marjorie Phelps, Helen Terry, and driver Horace J. Terry, who later would operate Terry's Gulf, Podunk's only gas station.

Hodgkins School.

A turn-of-the-century school bus. Will all of these children fit on board?

Podunk School, District #3. Originally located next to the Podunk Chapel, this structure was moved and converted to a residence in 1946 by James Rio. Mr. Rio occupies the building presently.

Podunk School, District #4. Still standing on West Sturbridge Road, this structure is now a private home.

Podunk District #3 schoolmates. From left to right are: (front row) Eugene Landrux, William Bancroft, Evelyn Landrux, and unknown; (middle row) unknown, Fred Hall, and Clarence Underwood; (back row) unknown and teacher Grace Bowen.

Podunk Road. This farm on Podunk Road is now the home of the McRaes, who operate the Podunk Kennels on the same site.

Howe Street. This farm on Howe Street is now the Lombardelli residence. For a long time it was known as the Willow Tree Farm, where many children learned to ride horses under the expert tutelage of Dot Steedman.

Podunk Chapel. This simple structure provided a humble gathering place for worshippers.

The McCrillis Farm on Howe Street.

A school picture from Podunk District #4. From left to right are: Agnes Wylie, May Haley, Mildred McDonald, George Haley, Miss Fisher (teacher), Goldie Wilson, ? Wylie, and Hugh Wylie. The group's casual pose is remarkable for Bullard's time.

Watching the trains go by. Two young fellows witness the thunderous passing of a Boston & Albany freight train. A good head of steam was necessary to get to the top of Charlton Hill! Since 1839, the children of East Brookfield have gladly coexisted with their life-size "train set." This scene is still repeated daily, though the engine now is a blue diesel. The effect is the same, however—it's the best show in town!

A view from the end of South Street, showing the North Brookfield branch line and the Parmenter brickyard. The white "smoke" at the center is steam from the train headed to North Brookfield.

The center of East Brookfield on a summer day, as seen from Vizard's Hill.

Looking west across the tranquil Lake Lashaway from behind the Lakeview House. The Baptist church steeple rises above the tree line.

Benoit's Blacksmith Shop. The boy in the photograph, keeping a close watch on Bill Bullard, is a young Ernest "Pet" Benoit. His dad is shoeing a horse. Pet took over the shop some years later and became noted in East Brookfield as the man who could fix anything, period. His shop was a magnet for generations of kids with broken bicycles and empty pockets. Pet ran the shop until the early 1980s and had the last working forge in the area. Those who visited the blacksmith shop knew that the place was magical and that Pet was a wizard of steel and iron, a town icon in green coveralls surrounded by sparks and fire.

Looking west on Main Street from the front of the Baptist church.

Our visit to East Brookfield ends with another look at an early form of transportation, in an era when getting there was truly half the fun!

Two
Brookfield

Central Street, looking east.

The Brookfield Congregational Church, in a view from Banister Common.

Central Street, looking west.

Brookfield Town Hall.

Three shops on Central Street. Shown here are Ford's Variety, Eaton's Pharmacy, and M. Donahue's Variety Store.

Central Street, near the corner of Sherman Street.

Central Street, looking east.

The Foster Moulton Shoe Company on Central Street. Gavitt Wire is now located on this site.

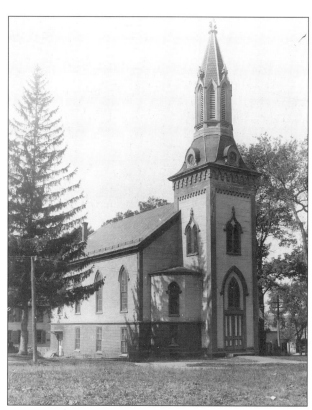

The Brookfield Methodist Church.

The Arcadia Inn at the corner of Common Street and the Post Road. The inn, built in 1810, was originally the home of Francis Howe.

River Street. The house on the right, on River Street, is now the home of Howard Glass.

Saint Mary's Catholic Church and rectory, as seen from Sherman Street.

Two views of Main Street, looking east and west, taken from the front of Joseph Guerin's blacksmith shop.

Lincoln Street, looking east, at the corner of Sherman Street.

River Street, looking south, near the corner of Lincoln Street.

Looking north on Common Street. In the summer this was a shady lane, indeed!

These two views of the Merrick Library illustrate the how small changes in lighting and camera angles can produce very different images.

The causeway, on what is now Route 148, approaching the bridge over the Quaboag River. The Ideal Paper Company, on Mill Street, is in the distance.

A closer view of the Ideal Paper Company.

Grove Street, looking east.

Looking north on River Street.

Travel between Worcester and Springfield was a major undertaking in the early 1900s. The Brookfield Inn was a splendid sight after a long, dusty trolley ride on the Post Road. It provided a pleasant night's rest for many who passed through the town.

A view of the Brookfield Inn and the Post Road.

Rest for the weary traveler. For many years the Arcadia Inn was an annex of the Brookfield Inn.

Outdoor recreation. A woman gets some rowing exercise on Lake Quaboag.

A pause for the camera. This well-dressed family posed for Bill Bullard during a lakeside outing.

The man and horsepower of the Brookfield Highway Department.

The Brookfield depot and freight house. A Boston & Albany train approaches the River Street overpass.

Two views, taken during different seasons, of Brookfield High School on River Street.

The Blanchard School on Maple Street. The school was named after Reverend Charles P. Blanchard in 1862. It was torn down in 1958. At this and many other sites Bill Bullard was responsible for introducing area youngsters to photography.

A rear view of the Blanchard School. The boys obviously have established a rapport with our photographer.

We pass the Brookfield Inn a final time on our way to historic West Brookfield.

Three
West Brookfield

The West Brookfield Town Hall.

Through the efforts of the Quaboag Historical Society, West Brookfield has long been aware of its place in history. Here is the stone monument marking the site of Fort Gilbert.

A prime location. The great Methodist evangelist George Whitefield gave a rousing oration from this rock on Foster Hill in 1740. The splendid view from the rock looks much the same today as it did then.

Indian Rock on Foster Hill, a landmark from the earliest days of the Quaboag Plantation.

A historic landmark. This fireplace was all that remained of the home of Judge Jedediah Foster, a West Brookfield veteran of the Revolutionary War. The house burned in 1901.

Let's stop for a chilled Moxie here on Main Street.

On the Common. The elementary school is on the far right. Turn to p. 125 for a present-day view of the same site.

The Merriam-Gilbert Library on Main Street.

Ye Olde Tavern. This establishment still offers food and drink in West Brookfield.

Main Street, looking west from the corner of School Street.

On the Common. This residence now houses the Varnum Funeral Home.

The West Brookfield First Congregational Church.

The West Brookfield Elementary School.

The Merriam-Webster Publishing Company on Main Street, birthplace of Webster's Dictionary. The Country Bank occupies this site today.

The Quaboag Corset Company on Pleasant Street.

A peaceful view of Lake Wickaboag.

The newspaper account read: "One person was killed and many injured in the above train wreck which took place November 9, 1907, in West Brookfield when the "Modoc" express #46 east bound ran into a west bound freight just opposite the old freight depot, a little west of the West Brookfield Station." According to the *North Brookfield Journal*, the express was one hour and forty minutes late; the engineer of the freight train had no knowledge that the Modoc was expected and was at a standstill when the heavy express engine—with six heavy cars—struck squarely head-on and completely demolished the buffet car at the head of the passenger train, killing the head brakeman.

"The interior of the dining car was a sight to behold," the *Journal* reported, "with crockery, glassware, and mirrors demolished. Breakfast was being served but few were in the car besides cooks and waiters. The engine crew of the freight train saw the oncoming express in time to jump to safety."

"The wreck was in almost the same spot where two tramps had recently been killed in a collision of freight trains. The curve west of the station was considered especially dangerous because belated trains from the west were in the habit of making up time across the Brookfield flats." This view from atop a freight car on an adjacent track illuminates the magnitude of the disaster.

A crowd forms. Rescuers and passengers gather at the head of the wrecked express.

The West Brookfield Station on a quiet day. Today the restored station serves as the West Brookfield Senior Center.

The interior of the wrecked buffet car. Soon after, wooden rail cars such as this were replaced with steel cars, which greatly reduced the destruction caused by accidents.

Going for a ride. Two West Brookfield gents take grandmother for a ride to North Brookfield in their new Tin Lizzy. Don't forget Rover!

Are we having fun yet? Farms provided plenty of work for everyone.

Four
North Brookfield

The North Brookfield Town Hall on Main Street.

The North Brookfield Town Hall with the awnings of summer in bloom.

Adams Block on Main Street.

Town hall on a Sunday morning: the awnings are rolled up and the town is quiet.

The Haston Free Public Library on Main Street.

Another view of the library on a bright, sunny day.

The B&R Rubber Company, now the Quaboag Rubber Company. It has been called the "Rubber Shop" by local workers for generations.

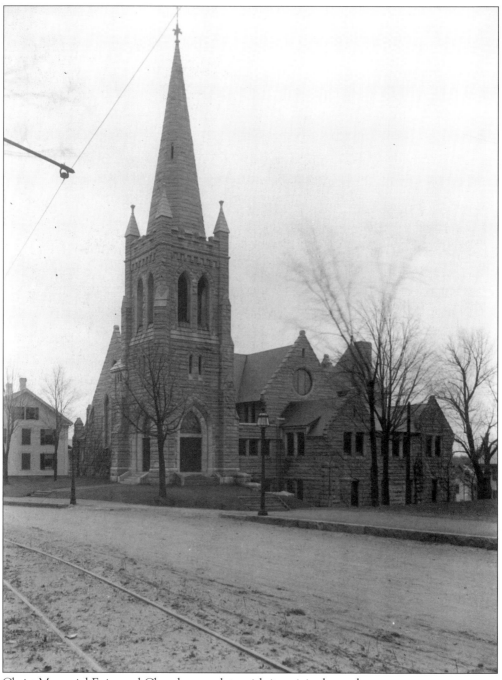

Christ Memorial Episcopal Church, complete with its original steeple.

Main Street, showing the Adams Block. The businesses there at the time were Blanchard's Grocery Store, Sam Clark's Jewelry Store, Morris Longly's Dry Goods Store, Gleason's Ice Cream Parlor, and Brainard Smith's Dry Goods Store.

Early transportation. Who needs a Harley when you have a gig? This was speedy travel for adventurous types.

Saint Joseph's Catholic Church on North Main Street.

U Will Call Again. The cobbler was an integral part of the community in an era when walking was the primary means of transportation. Bullard's artistic vision is evident in the composition of this unique photograph.

The Holmes Steamer, ready for any fire, is shown here in parade dress. The Brookfields' all-volunteer fire departments are still as rough and ready as their predecessors. The man on the right is believed to be Frank Foster.

The Holmes Steamer in full charge on Central Street. Boys run alongside this magnificent sight, and a Model T follows closely behind.

The Holmes Steamer. Pulled by a double team of horses, the steamer crosses New Haven Railroad tracks in Worcester en route to Green Hill Park for equipment demonstrations and muster competitions. We'd like to think the North Brookfield boys taught the city slickers a thing or two.

Milo Drake's farm on Brickyard Road. Milo used the wagon on his milk delivery route.

A Sunday ride with the ladies. Milo will drive.

The corner of Ward Street and Old East Brookfield Road.

The Haskell family at Sunnyside Farm on Old East Brookfield Road. The Joseph Dobeck family now calls this site their home.

A family affair. The Haskell children show off their pets. Typically, children gathered casually for Bullard's camera.

A one-room schoolhouse. Small district schoolhouses, like this one in North Brookfield, provided a solid education for rural Americans for more than two centuries. Students used what they learned to build the greatest country in the world. Remarkable inventions were created by imaginations stimulated in rustic one-room schools.

Two groups of young scholars, ready to learn. These kids would experience two world wars and the Great Depression, and many would live to see men fly to the moon.

A gathering of students. We are fortunate to know the names of most of these pupils because Alice (Rollins) Varney, grandmother-in-law of the author, can recall them personally. From left to right are: (front row) Antoinette Trudeau, May Mason, Lydia Potvin, Geraldine Jean, Oleida Potvin, Margaret Doane, Muriel Cannon, and unknown; (middle row) unknown, William Fullam, Carroll Varney, Leon Prescott, Guy Wilkins, Emily Hack, unknown, and Geraldine Brown; (third row) unknown, Howard Dooley, three unknown boys, and Fred Grainger.

North Brookfield High. A high school class poses formally for William Bullard, whose prints would provide the students with lifetime memories. Alice Varney still has hers.

Living well. Everyone could own a home thanks to J.W. Wilbur, the greatest land company on earth, whose agent is shown here visiting North Brookfield.

Camping out. A guy could get away from the noise of younger siblings in his own army surplus tent, complete with floor and brass bed. This may have been the birth of recreational camping in our area.

The farm of Benjamin Banks. Evelyn Banks is in the yard with her doll carriage.

A rustic scene. The Banks Farm would become Brookfield Orchards, North Brookfield's top harvest-time attraction. The orchard draws thousands of visitors each year.

This farm on Shore Road would one day become part of Camp Atwater. It still stands today.

The beauty and composition of this photograph testifies to Bullard's skill. The field in the foreground is now the site of Camp Atwater.

Strawberry time at Milo Drake's. The giggling girls have been charmed into posing in strawberry crates.

Hillsville Road. This home on Hillsville Road is now occupied by Frank Hubacz.

On the farm. A dairy farmer poses with his best bovines.

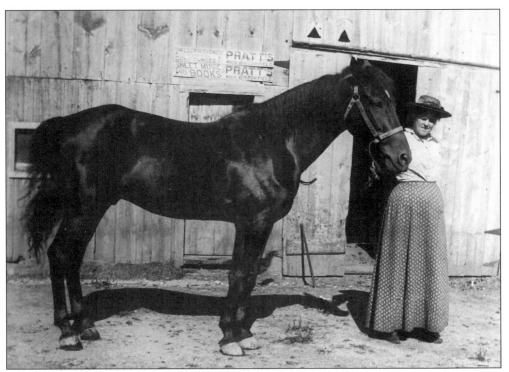

Equine care. This North Brookfield girl is obviously proud of her beautiful horse.

Time off. Workers of the North Brookfield Railroad take a break with Bill Bullard. The branch line passed near the Bullard family farm.

Boss and crew. A well-dressed track foreman and two of his workers take a rest on their Fairbanks-Morse hand pumper before a quick ride to East Brookfield.

Steam train. This is the only known photograph from this era of a steam train on the North Brookfield branch. The Brickyard Road crossing is just ahead of the engine.

Francis Drake. This powerful portrait of Francis Drake was taken in his barn. This friend of Mr. Bullard was a well-known producer of melons at Drake's Garden in East Brookfield.

Prize squash. A small boy marvels at the produce at the Drake Farm.

Happy times at the Bullard family farm. That's William in the wheelbarrow.

A Bullard family portrait spanning four generations. From left to right are: (front row) Brenda Bullard (wife of Marcus), baby Robert, grandmother Sarah Bullard, and mother Ellen Bullard; (back row) Ellen's son Marcus, daughter Bertie, and son William.

On the farm. Marcus Bullard demonstrates a corn grinder for the family.

Brenda Bullard with daughter Evelyn. Evelyn died in 1994.

The Bullard family home on Bullard Road in North Brookfield.

The interior of the Bullards' home at the turn of the century.

A bountiful crop. Brenda and Ellen Bullard enjoy the harvest, while Charlie and Marcus do some heavy lifting. Family portraits at this time were usually formal, so we're fortunate to have a look at these family members just being themselves.

Preparing kindling. The family works together at the woodpile.

Country charm. William, Bertie, and their grandmother Sarah bare their soles for the camera, probably operated with a timer.

Plenty for everyone. Apples are in season at the Bullard family orchard.

A simple life. William Bullard poses with his niece Evelyn and nephew Robert. The pose is characteristic of Bill's personality, since he frequently appeared as a relaxed and friendly observer in the background of country life. Perhaps this photograph represents Bill as he would most like himself to be remembered.

Quitting time. At the extreme left, Charlie Bullard leans on a barrel, next to the family's neighbor. William Bullard poses with his dog next to Marcus, Brenda, and Ellen Bullard. Some laundry items are drying in the wind, and the family appears to be breathing a well-earned sigh of relief after completing the day's chores.

The family gathers. From left to right are: (front row) Ellen, Robert, and Brenda; (back row) Charlie, William, and Marcus. Charlie Bullard, as previously noted, was responsible for preserving Bill's glass plate negatives for forty years after his brother's death.

An eerie self-portrait. This is as close as we get to having a picture of William Bullard at work. His camera can be seen in the mirror over the fireplace, without any trace of the photographer himself. Because of the long exposure time required in photography during Bullard's lifetime, it may be assumed that Bill was able to leave the scene before his own image was registered.

A precious pose. Dorothy Bullard poses for Uncle Bill. The photographer's talent for posing presumably fidgety young children was truly remarkable.

The North Brookfield District #8 School. Located on Brickyard Road, this building was where the Bullards were educated. Photographs of schoolchildren were often taken outside because of the dangers associated with early flash photography.

The Brookfield Congregational Church in 1996.

The North Brookfield Town Hall in 1996.

The West Brookfield Common in 1996. Paul and Thomas LeBeau dutifully recreate a Bullard classic scene for their photographer father, Dennis LeBeau.

Our visit to the Brookfields ends back in East Brookfield at Lashaway Park. At the time of this photograph, the earliest stirrings of the Jazz Age were beginning. Numerous trolley lines enabled touring groups such as this one to travel to small towns across America.

My Album's open! come and see!
What! won't you waste a line on me?
Write, but a thought, a word or two,
That memory my revert to you.

Live for those that love you,
For those whose hearts are true
For the heaven that smiles above you
And the good you may do.

When the name that I write here is dim on the page,
And the leaves of your album is yellow with age
Still think of me kindly, and do not forget
That wherever I am, I remember you yet

When years and months have glided by,
And on this page you cast your eye,
Remember 'twas a friend sincere
That left this kind remembrance here.

This poem was handwritten in a notebook that belonged to William Bullard. It seems almost as though he had this book in mind when he wrote it, and it seems an appropriate way to conclude our passage through the life and time of this humble photographer. May we remember fondly the life of this great artist, whose career was tragically cut short.

Acknowledgments

Many people shared their recollections of the past with me over the course of this project. Mrs. Sylvia Vivier and her son Francis provided vivid memories and identifications of their former neighbors, the Bullards.

Brookfield's own Peter Terry is a walking encyclopedia of Brookfield lore. He and his friends, Bob and Cindy Sheppard of Hometown Antiques in West Brookfield, were very helpful.

In North Brookfield, Sheila Buzzell, Reedy Nealer Jr., and George Hanson helped us access town clerk and assessors records from days of old. Buddy Lane of the Cemetery Commission led us to the final resting place of the Bullard family in North Brookfield.

Franklin and Barbara Drake helped to identify people and places in photographs of East Brookfield.

On the technical side of things, David Guertin and Paul LeBeau provided enthusiastic darkroom assistance during the printing of Bullard's glass plate negatives.

Special thanks go to editor Bob Smith of Spencer, retired from the *Detroit Free Press*, and Russell Powell, formerly of Rice Corner Road, Brookfield, who wrote the introduction. Pam LeBeau offered her typing skills on a moment's notice, while her grandmother, Alice Varney, often brought pictures to life with personal memories.

I would also like to thank Jamie Carter of Arcadia for her enthusiasm and expertise.

Finally, I am of course most grateful to Charlie Bullard and Frank Gaudette for preserving the historic and poignant images of William Bullard's life work.

Dennis LeBeau, 1996